IMAGES
of America

KENOSHA'S JEFFERY
AND RAMBLER
AUTOMOBILES

A 1902 Rambler is pictured on a sunny afternoon drive in the country. Americans came to love the advent of the automobile age. It gave them the personal freedom to travel farther in a day than ever before, without being tied to the railroads. For some, it also allowed more serious courting away from prying eyes. (Author's collection.)

ON THE COVER: One of the earliest and most successful cars of the 20th century was the 1902 Rambler, seen here. At the controls—in this case a steering tiller—is George W. Mason, chief executive officer of Nash-Kelvinator Corporation, a successor to the firm that first built the Rambler, the Thomas B. Jeffery Company of Kenosha, Wisconsin. Next to Mason, doffing his hat, is Nash sales vice president Henry Clay Doss. This photograph was taken around 1948 using a vintage Rambler owned by the company. (Author's collection.)

IMAGES
of America

KENOSHA'S JEFFERY
AND RAMBLER
AUTOMOBILES

Patrick Foster
Foreword by Chris Allen, Kenosha History Center

ARCADIA
PUBLISHING

Published by Arcadia Publishing
Charleston, South Carolina

Library of Congress Control Number: 2017963155

For all general information, please contact Arcadia Publishing:
Telephone 843-853-2070
Fax 843-853-0044
E-mail sales@arcadiapublishing.com
For customer service and orders:
Toll-Free 1-888-313-2665

Visit us on the Internet at www.arcadiapublishing.com

*This book is dedicated to my best friends, Mike Sheldon,
Jim McGuire, Leo Carroll, and Mike Rice.*

CONTENTS

FOREWORD

To this day, when a Rambler drives down the road in Kenosha, Wisconsin, one can still hear the words "I built that car" from onlookers. Not only are the words spoken, they are spoken with the utmost pride. Kenosha is an auto town. It has been since Thomas B. Jeffery sold his rights to his bicycle company in Chicago, Illinois, and moved to Kenosha, Wisconsin, in 1900 to open up a new automobile company.

The fact that Kenosha is still an auto town, when a car has not rolled off the line since 1988, should tell you something. It is not that the town has not moved on. It has more to do with the fact that when an industry is in a town for over a century, it becomes intertwined with the town. The "plant," as everyone called it, provided jobs for generations of Kenoshans. In addition to working directly for Jeffery (or later Nash, AMC, or Chrysler), the industry created many ancillary jobs as well. Jobs working at the docks, railyards, transporting business, and others were plentiful.

Jeffery was able to lay the groundwork for many successful years of automobile production in Kenosha. To this day, if you talk to many Kenoshans, they have memories of going to work at the plant. To some, that plant was Chrysler; to some, AMC; a few worked there in the Nash years; and some remember stories that their relatives told about the early years at Jeffery. The common thread in all of the stories, however, is the pride that each worker took in producing one of the finest automobiles in the world and being part of a company that was innovative and always trying to produce a quality machine, not just a lot of cars.

Often, Thomas B. Jeffery is either overlooked or forgotten as one of the great industrialists of his time. Even in Kenosha, birthplace of the Jeffery Rambler, AMC, Nash, and Chrysler are mentioned in conversation more often than Jeffery. Obviously, time is a factor; with the last Jeffery rolling off the line in 1916, there are not too many cars that were made by the T.B. Jeffery Company still on the road. More people recognize the Rambler name as the car that Nash made. It is important to remember that without Jeffery, Nash would probably not have made its home in Kenosha and quite possibly would never have had the ability to grow into the company that it eventually did.

Jeffery should be remembered not only for his many innovations in his field but also for laying the foundation for a thriving automobile industry in Kenosha, ultimately providing thousands of jobs and brighter futures for Kenoshans. When T.B. Jeffery died in 1910, Henry Ford wrote a letter to Thomas's son Charles Jeffery offering his condolences. In the letter, he notes that he "fully appreciate[s] the distinct loss he will be to you all as well as to the Industry in which we are all engaged."

When one thinks of American automobiles, Detroit is usually synonymous with that thought. However, another Midwestern city was producing automobiles one year prior to Ford in Detroit. When Thomas B. Jeffery chose Kenosha as the city in which he would open up his new automobile factory, he planted the seed that grew into 110-plus years of auto making, providing vehicles, jobs, and memories for countless Americans. Jeffery's contributions to the automobile industry were great, but they pale in comparison to the impact the company made on the city of Kenosha. Kenosha has a car legacy, started in 1900 by Jeffery and continued by Nash, American Motors, and eventually, Chrysler. The fabric of the industry is still woven into the city.

Chris Allen is the executive director of the Kenosha County Historical Society. The historical society operates the Kenosha History Center museum, which features an annual car exhibit in its Rambler Legacy Gallery. In addition, the history center hosts the Kenosha Homecoming Car Show every two to three years in which the cars that were made in Kenosha and that made Kenosha return home. The 2017 show saw 937 vehicles in attendance.

ACKNOWLEDGMENTS

Most of the photographs and images used in this book came from the world-famous Patrick R. Foster Historical Collection, a large, working archive dedicated to the preservation and dissemination of historical information about American Motors, its predecessor companies, and subsidiary and related firms. The Patrick R. Foster Historical Collection is the foremost American Motors archive in the world. Additional photographs were provided by Chuck Heide, and the author is grateful for his help. Heide's father worked for the Thomas B. Jeffery Company back in its heyday.

The author would like to thank Chris Allen and Cynthia Nelson of the Kenosha History Center for their help. He would also like to thank the men and women of Arcadia Publishing for allowing him to bring to the world a book dedicated to the early Rambler and Jeffery cars and trucks. It was only through the help of all these special people that this special book was made possible.

Thomas B. Jeffery was an inventor and builder. Over his long career, he manufactured baby carriages, bicycles, tires, automobiles, trucks, and more. His contribution to America's industrial history was great, and the companies that succeeded him include Nash Motors, Nash-Kelvinator, American Motors, and Jeep.

INTRODUCTION

Tom Jeffery was an immigrant, a nobody, just one of the hundreds of thousands of people who left their homes and familiar surroundings to journey by ship to America in search of a better life. He had heard that America was a land of opportunity that welcomed newcomers to earn a place in a young, growing country. America was a place where dreams could come true.

In 1863, during the middle of the American Civil War, 18-year-old Thomas Buckland Jeffery decided to leave his native England. Booking passage to America, he became part of the great wave of immigrants traveling to the New World. Upon his arrival, young Tom somehow managed to avoid the army recruiters as well as the scores of timid civilians hoping to entice immigrants into joining the army in their place. Wartime rules allowed states to offer large cash bounties to lure young men into the army and also allowed those wealthy enough to afford it to pay for a substitute to take their place in the service.

However, young Tom Jeffery had already decided to move on to Chicago. He had been tolerably well educated and had valuable skills, having served as an apprentice in an instrument maker's shop in Plymouth, Devonshire. He had an uncommon aptitude for mechanical work and was anxious to put that skill to good use in his new country. An acquaintance later recalled that young Tom had a hunger to make things.

In Chicago, he got a job making telescopes, microscopes, and other complex scientific instruments. America was good to Tom; he earned a good wage and was able to set aside enough money to eventually open his own shop, where he built patent models for inventors who were trying to get their inventions patented. It took a high level of skill to do such painstaking work, and Tom earned a good living. At age 29, he married Kate Elizabeth Wray, who over time blessed him with four children: Charles, Harold, Eva Mable, and Florence. Before long, Tom expanded his shop to include the manufacture of baby carriages. In the mid-1870s, he invented a foot-propelled railroad velocipede for railroad workers to travel the rails. The conventional railroad hand-trucks at the time used a sort of rowing seesaw lever that was hard on the back. Jeffery's invention instead used a bicycle-pedal action.

In 1878, Tom Jeffery made a return trip to England, where he spotted a penny-farthing bicycle and immediately recognized that it represented an opportunity for him to expand his business. He ordered parts to be shipped home to Chicago and, by 1879, had his own bicycle ready for production. In honor of his new country, he called it the American.

In time, Tom realized he needed help. He loved his factory, and he loved to tinker and to build things, but the paperwork end of the business bored him. In 1881, he formed a partnership with an old schoolmate named R. Phillip Gormully to create Gormully & Jeffery Manufacturing Company. The men were hard workers, and they made an excellent product, and in a few years' time, their company became the second largest bicycle manufacturer in America. Phil Gormully took care of the paperwork and financial side of the business, leaving Tom free to run his factory while also creating new products. By 1891, this included the revolutionary clincher tire, which made changing tires much easier. A new firm, G&J Tire Company, was incorporated to manufacture Jeffery's tire. With two highly successful businesses, the two friends grew wealthy.

Along the way, the bicycles were given a new name: Rambler. Success followed success until 1899, when Phil Gormully died and Tom Jeffery, probably realizing that the bicycle boom was about to end, sold the Gormully & Jeffery Manufacturing Company to Col. Albert Pope, the power behind the notorious American Bicycle Company, which consolidated some 41 such firms into a competition-killing monopoly.

The following year, a restless 55-year-old Tom Jeffery purchased a huge factory building in Kenosha, Wisconsin, with the idea of starting a new company to manufacture an entirely new product while providing an opportunity for his two boys, now reaching manhood, to have a company to run when he was no longer able to run it himself. His son Charles was interested in automobiles. Tom realized that would be a good product for a growing America. Little did he know how large his company would become or how important it would prove to his adopted country.

Indeed, this little automobile company would eventually grow into the largest corporation in Wisconsin and among the 80 largest companies in America, employing thousands of people in good jobs at good wages. All because one English teenager decided that America was truly, as it had always been said, the land of opportunity. May it always be so.

One

1897–1901

In 1897, Thomas B. Jeffery, the immigrant English inventor, and his son Charles built this experimental automobile in the machine shop of his bicycle factory in Chicago, Illinois. He called it a Rambler, after the bicycles he had been producing since 1879. This is the only known photograph of Jeffery's first attempt at designing an automobile. He and Charles would do a great deal of experimenting and perfecting before introducing their first production model.

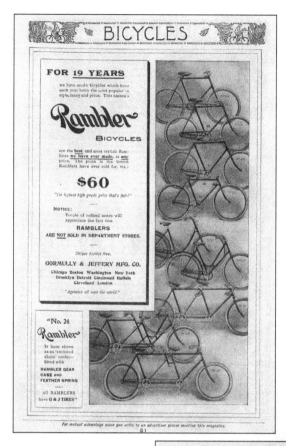

Before he entered the automobile manufacturing field, Jeffery produced bicycles. This advertisement from 1898 illustrates some of the numerous models of Rambler bicycles that the Gormully & Jeffery Manufacturing Company offered that year. By this point, the company was the second largest bicycle manufacturer in America.

One of Tom Jeffery's greatest inventions was the clincher tire, which he developed in 1891. It made changing or repairing a bicycle or (a bit later) automobile tire much easier. The idea took fire with the public, so partners Phillip Gormully and Thomas Jeffery formed the G&J Tire Company to produce them. Years later, the company was sold to the US Rubber Company.

These three early ads for Rambler bicycles emphasize that bicycling is good exercise while reassuring people that it is also safe—some potential buyers actually worried about traveling at speed on what seemed such an unstable device! As the ad on the right notes, Gormully and Jeffery were leaders in the burgeoning bicycle industry.

In the fall of 1900, Charles Jeffery and his father built two additional experimental automobiles, a Runabout and a Stanhope. They were exhibited to the public in September at the Chicago International Exhibition. Then, in November, they appeared at the first New York Auto Show, where they were referred to as the G&J, Rambler, or Hydrocar. Shown here is the Runabout.

Here is the Stanhope model, also produced in 1900. It is identical to the Runabout except for the folding top, which provided a measure of protection from the weather. The two cars were powered by two-cylinder, water-cooled engines (probably the reason why they were sometimes referred to as the Hydrocar) mounted up front. This went against the usual American practice of placing the engine under the seat and thus was considered radical for the time.

After viewing the two experimental Ramblers at the auto shows, the public naturally expected to see production begin in short order. However, the Jefferys were not satisfied with their car just yet. In 1901, Charles Jeffery built this fourth experimental car, known as the Model A, in Kenosha, Wisconsin. This car featured left-hand steering, a water-cooled, front-mounted engine, and a steering wheel, all very advanced features. Tom Jeffery decided it was too radical to offer as their first automobile.

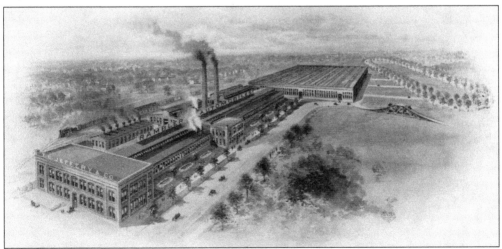

The above experimental car was the first to be built at the family's newly purchased factory in Kenosha, Wisconsin. The previous experimental jobs had been built in Chicago. Formerly home to Sterling Bicycles, Jeffery's new plant was quite large and eminently suited to large-scale production of automobiles. This picture is undated but is believed to be of a later date, probably around 1907, after several expansions needed to increase production capacity.

Looking quite trim and modern compared to the previous experimental Ramblers is this Model B, produced in 1901. It is believed to be the fifth experimental car built by the Jefferys. It was powered by a water-cooled, two-cylinder engine and appears to have a floor-shifted transmission, judging by the lever next to the steering column.

Here, the Rambler Model B undergoes engineering tests on the roads around Kenosha. To test its hauling ability, a wagon loaded with lumber has been hitched up, and three workers also climbed aboard to add some weight—and probably to get a little air as well. The 1901 Wisconsin State Fair is advertised on the billboard in the background.

16

Two

1902–1905

The first production Rambler was the Model C Runabout shown here, which followed the experimental Models A and B. Unlike those automobiles, the Model C featured a one-cylinder, water-cooled engine mounted underneath the vehicle body. Bore and stroke were 4½ by 6 inches. Although various historical publications list 4, 8, and 12 horsepower, the author believes 4 horsepower is the correct figure. The wheelbase was a short 72 inches. Steering was by tiller, and the driver sat on the right-hand side of the vehicle, as was the custom in those early days of the automobile. The transmission was a simple planetary type, with a chain drive to the rear axle. The first Rambler was sold on March 1, 1902 during the Chicago Auto Show. The vehicle was priced at a modest $750. Rambler quickly earned a reputation as a high-quality car at a very reasonable price. The name chosen for the new business was Thomas B. Jeffery & Co.

MODEL D

The 1902 Rambler Model D was like the C but also included a hand-buffed folding leather top, rubber side curtains, and a storm apron for weather protection. It sold for $825. The crank handle on the side of the body is for starting the car, which the driver could do from his seat if he wished. The earliest Ramblers were equipped with wire wheels and no fenders, though later in the season, spoke wheels and fenders would be introduced. Note that this car has been fitted with gas headlamps—the storage tank can be seen mounted just behind the seat.

This is a view inside the Thomas B. Jeffery & Co. factory in Kenosha in 1902, when the first Ramblers were being produced. At this point, the cars are still being supplied with wire wheels. The production sequence involved teams of men assembling the chassis in one area while other produced the bodies in another, after which the two would be joined together. This was quite different from the assembly line approach that would come into practice in the coming decade.

Reliability was a common problem with early cars, and automakers went out of their way to convince potential buyers that their product could be counted on to deliver good service. The best way to prove the reliability of a car was to enter it in a race or, as seen here, a reliability run. This particular event is the 1902 New York–to–Boston Reliability Run, held from October 9 to 15. At the tiller is Arthur Gardiner, and his passenger is Charles Jeffery, designer of the car, whose father was Thomas B. Jeffery. The Rambler cars quickly gained a reputation for outstanding reliability.

Here is another 1902 Rambler Model C, this time equipped with headlamps. Most history books claim that 1,500 Ramblers were produced for 1902, but there is evidence that the number might actually have been 400 cars instead. This is based on a statement reportedly made by Thomas B. Jeffery in the December 30, 1908, issue of *Horseless Age* magazine. However, 1902 models have been located with serial numbers higher than 400, so the question is not yet completely resolved.

This factory press release photograph of a 1902 Rambler illustrates changes that were made during the first year of production. The wire wheels have been replaced by stronger wood spoke wheels, and fenders are now included, though they probably were an extra cost item. The seat appears to be completely different as well. The Model Cs, apparently, were all painted Brewster green with red chassis paint.

This side view of a later 1902 Rambler clearly shows the spoke wheels and fenders and the change in the seat to a slightly more integrated design. Note, too, that the rear of the body is rounder and now includes cooling slots for the engine. The owner, Dr. George B. Crissman, is seen here with his fiancée during a pleasure drive in Fort Collins, Colorado. He has added headlamps to the car, which are covered in this photograph, and a centrally mounted front warning light.

The limitations of the Rambler's single-seat design soon became apparent. In this photograph, the owner of the Model C has added a rear seat to hold his wife and mother-in-law, while his daughter rides up front with him.

Charles Jeffery and his father were astute businessmen and recognized that many owners would need to carry more than one passenger. They mocked up a four-place Rambler Model C by mounting a small bench seat over the front storage box. However, this placement tended to block the driver's view when the seat was occupied, so the idea never was put into production. The two men began working on larger, roomier models.

In later years, Nash-Kelvinator Company, which was a successor to the Thomas B. Jeffery Company, purchased a 1902 Rambler Model C for sentimental reasons and to use for promotional purposes. This particular car was treated to a full restoration that, unfortunately, included the inauthentic paint job seen here, complete with stylish graphics highlighting the Rambler name.

This photograph, taken outside the Nash-Kelvinator headquarters garage some time during the early 1950s, shows an early Rambler that was owned by the company. It may even be the same car as shown above prior to its restoration. The occasion was a factory service training school held for dealer mechanics. The driver is not identified but is probably either a Nash dealer or a mid-level Nash executive.

Here is the basic Rambler runabout for 1903. Now dubbed the Model E, this one has been fitted with a rear seat, and the owner has taken off the lid for the front storage box in order to seat two small children. The 1903 models featured a wheelbase lengthened to 78 inches. The engine bore was increased to five inches, boosting output to six horsepower. Note the steering wheel, which entered production some time during the model year. This year, the company hired a new test driver, Fred Duesenberg, who would later develop one of the greatest cars of all time.

The Rambler Models C and D were renamed the Models E and F for 1903. This photograph, which was provided by American Motors, shows an early 1903 Rambler Model F Touring Car. This is known to be an early illustration of the 1903 model because it still uses a tiller for steering. Note, too, how the design of the seat and top appear different from the 1902 models.

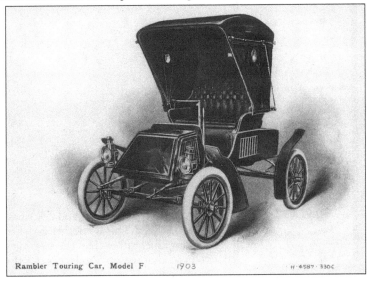

Rambler Touring Car, Model F   1903   H·4587·330C

Rambler popularity continued to grow as its reputation for reliability spread. This young fellow is giving two ladies a drive around town in his 1903 Rambler Model E Runabout. Note the brick roadway, a sure sign that he is near a town and not out in the country. This photograph was provided by Chuck Heide, so it may have been taken near Kenosha. On the back of the photograph is a note that reads, "Smiles on the kid's faces—not on the mother-in-law to be!" (Courtesy of Chuck Heide.)

A primitive method of locomotion used in Ecuador, South America.

Simplicity
Durability
Reliability

are the three cardinal virtues in motor-carriage construction. You will find them in their highest development and efficiency in the

Rambler
Touring Car

Built for practical, every-day service, on all kinds of roads, in all kinds of weather, the Rambler has proved its genuine merit under all conditions. Its many points of superiority are stated in detail in our

Complete Illustrated Catalogue

mailed free on request. The best grade of materials, backed by the highest class of skilled labor, make the Rambler a guarantee of quality.

MODEL F (like cut)
Thomas B. Jeffery & Co. $750.00
Kenosha, - - - - Wis.

This ad from 1903 shows and describes the Rambler Model F for that year. This is another early model, showing the steering tiller rather than the steering wheel used on later vehicles that season. Production for the year totaled 1,350 cars. Reportedly all the 1903 models were painted carmine red.

Here is an elegant 1904 Rambler Model L Surrey complete with wicker picnic baskets and a fixed roof panel for protection from the sun. Power was provided by a 25-horsepower, two-cylinder engine.

This racy-looking number is the Rambler Model K Touring Car for 1904. It is equipped for night use, with dual cowl lamps and a large central headlamp.

This photograph provides a rare scene inside Tom Jeffery's factory in Kenosha, where factory hands are working on the 1904 Ramblers. Note the larger size of the chassis and the steering wheels mounted on the right-hand side—typical practice in America back before the industry settled on left-hand steering. A factory worker explained that each newly built engine was broken in by using power from another engine to turn it. That may be what is seen here. Note the chain running from the flywheel to a shaft underneath the test stand. (Courtesy of Chuck Heide.)

One of the most popular cars of 1904 was this handsome Rambler Model L, a five-passenger automobile on an 84-inch wheelbase. Its motive power was a Jeffery-produced two-cylinder engine that generated 16 horsepower driving through a planetary transmission connected to the rear axle via chain drive. Cooling, as per standard Rambler practice, was by thermo syphon. Weighing just 1,725 pounds, this style of car was capable of speeds up to 40 miles per hour. These automobiles were finished in a carmine red color scheme. Note the tall windshield, surrey-type roof, and wicker picnic baskets, all of which made this an ideal car for a ride in the country.

Thomas B. Jeffery & Co. greatly expanded its model line for 1904 with the addition of the single-cylinder Model G priced at $750, single-cylinder Model H at $850, two-cylinder Model K at $1,200, and two-cylinder Model L at $1,359. In addition to the models pictured here, there was a two-passenger Model J priced at $1,100, the Model E, now priced at $650, and a delivery wagon known as the Type 1. Production for the year rose sharply to 2,342 vehicles.

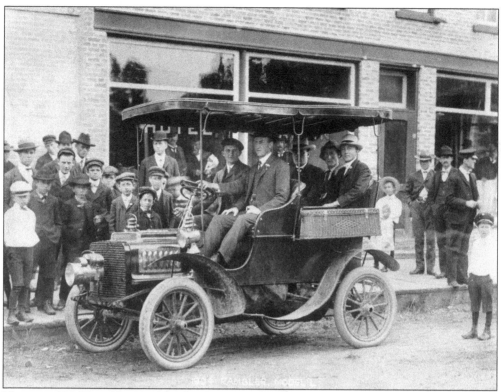

Here is a 1904 Rambler Model L loaded up and out for a drive. Note that it carries its full complement of five passengers. This well-equipped machine has the standard cowl lamps plus a center headlamp and the popular twin picnic baskets. The surrey top protected passengers from the sun and could be supplemented with side curtains. This year, the company began publication of the *Rambler Magazine*. Filled with stories of owners' travels and adventures in their automobiles, it was one of the first owner-focused publications in the auto industry.

This rare photograph shows a 1904 Rambler Type 1 Delivery Wagon, the first commercial vehicle produced by Thomas B. Jeffery & Co. Priced at $850, the Type 1 could carry two people and up to 500 pounds of merchandise. Carrying space was two cubic yards. The seven-horsepower, single-cylinder engine could propel the car up to 25 miles per hour. Fuel economy was good and, unlike a horse, the Rambler needed no fuel when not in use. The finish color was Rambler carmine.

Here is a 1904 Rambler runabout believed to be a Model J. The J is similar to the Model G in appearance, but the two vary quite a bit mechanically. The Model G is a single-cylinder car riding an 81-inch wheelbase, while the Model J is powered by a two-cylinder engine and rides an 84-inch wheelbase. The Model J also has longer springs for a smoother ride. Although both models were normally two-seaters, the body framing included iron reinforcement so that a two-passenger tonneau seat could easily be added later if the owner so desired.

The popular Rambler Model L for 1904 was an ideal touring car back in the day when automobiles were seen primarily as pleasure vehicles useful for drives into the country. It was able to carry a driver and four passengers at speeds up to 40 miles per hour, and a tank of gas allowed up to 150 miles of touring, which was important in an age when gasoline stations were few and far between.

Debuting for 1905 was the new Rambler Surrey Type One, seen here with owner L.L. Peddinghaus at the wheel. Similar in concept to the earlier Model L, the Surrey Type One was powered by a two-cylinder engine of 18 horsepower, two more than the L, and rode a longer 96-inch wheelbase. Peddinghaus was an amateur photographer who took this photograph using an automatic lens timer; some years, later the photograph was sent to American Motors, where it was included in some editions of its *Family Album*.

With the ability to travel greater distances in a day than ever before, early motorists needed road signs to help them find their way. To help its owners—and everyone else who traveled—Thomas B. Jeffery & Co. launched a program in which it erected signs throughout the countryside. In this photograph, workers set up a sign stating that Milwaukee is 27.5 miles ahead.

This advertisement from the November 9, 1904, issue of *Horseless Age* talks about a race held in Rockford, Illinois, in which a 1904 Rambler bested a competitor's 1905 car, even though the Rambler had but a two-cylinder engine while the other car was a four-cylinder! Note at the bottom of the ad that the company lists branch offices in New York, Boston, Chicago, and Philadelphia, in addition to its main office and factory in Kenosha, Wisconsin.

Here is an excellent photograph of a typical 1905 Rambler Surrey Type One. As can be seen, it was a fairly large car for the era, capable of carrying four or five people in comfort. Note that the driver has his hand on the steering wheel while also depressing the brass ring immediately below the wheel. That ring is actually the throttle control. The foot pedals seen are for the brakes and for controlling the different gears in the planetary gearbox. Note, too, how plush and well-padded the seats are. The Type One Surrey sold for $1,350.

This is the 1905 Rambler Surrey Type Two, shown for comparison with the Type One just above. The differences in wheelbase can easily be seen; the rear compartment is larger, as is the small access door to it. This car also has the full glass windshield, as well as the surrey top with roll-down side curtains for weather protection. The price as shown was $2,000.

Rambler

SURREY TYPE ONE
18 horse power, $1350

The *operation* of this vehicle is both *simple* and *natural*. The ignition of the spark is entirely automatic. The brakes are operated by pedals, not by levers. With the steering wheel and throttle, attached to it, operable by one hand, the other hand is always free to manage the clutches by the single lever, and no confusion is possible. ❡ Other models $750, $850, $2000 and $3000. ❡*Immediate delivery.*

Main Office and Factory; Kenosha, Wisconsin. E.R. Cumbe, 1618-20 Court Place, Denver, Colorado, W.K. Cowan, 830-34 South Broadway, Los Angeles, California, Rambler Automobile Agency; Tenth and Market Streets, San Francisco, California.

This ad for the 1905 Rambler Surrey Type One used an antique typeface. The Rambler logo at top was the same one used on the Rambler bicycles. In retrospect, using the Rambler nameplate rather than Jeffery or G&J made the most sense, because Rambler was one of the best-known and most respected names in bicycles and had been for years.

33

Here is another rare peek inside the Thomas B. Jeffery & Co. factory in Kenosha around 1905. Tom Jeffery was a man who loved his factory and insisted on only the best equipment and the finest workmanship. To ensure quality, Jeffery made nearly every part that went into the Ramblers, including frames, bodies, engines, and axles.

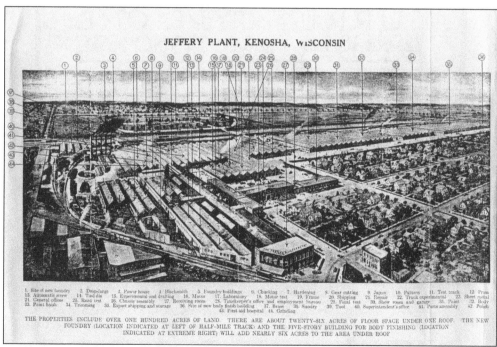

JEFFERY PLANT, KENOSHA, WISCONSIN

1. Site of new foundry   2. Drop-forge   3. Power house   4. Blacksmith   5. Foundry buildings   6. Chucking   7. Hardening   8. Gear cutting   9. Japan   10. Pattern   11. Test track   12. Press
13. Automatic screw   14. Tool die   15. Experimental and drafting   16. Motor   17. Laboratory   18. Motor test   19. Frame   20. Shipping   21. Repair   22. Truck experimental   23. Sheet metal
24. General offices   25. Road test   26. Chassis assembly   27. Receiving room   28. Timekeeper's office and employment bureau   29. Final test   30. Show room and garage   31. Paint   32. Body
33. Paint finish   34. Trimming   35. Export shipping and storage   36. Site of new body finish building   37. Brass   38. Sundry   39. Tool   40. Superintendent's office   41. Parts assembly   42. Polish
43. First aid hospital   44. Grinding

THE PROPERTIES INCLUDE OVER ONE HUNDRED ACRES OF LAND. THERE ARE ABOUT TWENTY-SIX ACRES OF FLOOR SPACE UNDER ONE ROOF. THE NEW FOUNDRY (LOCATION INDICATED AT LEFT OF HALF-MILE TRACK) AND THE FIVE-STORY BUILDING FOR BODY FINISHING (LOCATION INDICATED AT EXTREME RIGHT) WILL ADD NEARLY SIX ACRES TO THE AREA UNDER ROOF

The quality of this picture is not as good as the author would like, but it has been included to give the reader some idea of the magnitude of the Jeffery works. By 1905, the property itself was over 100 acres and included about 26 acres under roof. The company had its own forge shop, body plant, trimming and painting facility, and engine plant, not to mention its own test track plus a showroom and offices. In fact, the Jeffery factory was the second largest automobile plant in America.

Rambler

Easiest to Operate
—Safest to Drive

There is no complicated system of levers on the Rambler. Every part is as simple as the Rambler control, here shown.

Below the steering wheel on the Rambler is the throttle, which can be tilted by the fingers to increase or decrease the speed of the car at will.

Every forward movement of the car, from highest speed to full stop, can be controlled without moving the hand from the steering wheel.

The Rambler catalogue explains in detail why the Rambler is the car for you to buy. It is mailed on request.

Surrey, Type One, $1,350.00 Other models, $750.00 to $3,000.00.

Thos. B. Jeffery & Co., Main Office and Factory, Kenosha, Wis., U. S. A.

Branches:—Boston; 145 Columbus Ave.   Chicago, 302-304 Wabash Ave.   Philadelphia, 242 N. Broad St.
New York Agency, 134 W. 38th St.   Agencies in other leading cities.

One unique feature of the early Rambler was the steering-column-mounted throttle. With this, the driver could control the speed of the car without taking his hands off the steering wheel, unlike most cars of the day, which used a dash-mounted pull throttle to control speed.

1905 Rambler

This drawing of a 1905 Rambler Surrey Type Two was done in the 1960s or 1970s by American Motors, a successor to the Thomas B. Jeffery Company, to provide the public with a greater understanding of how long the firm had been in business. The wood-framed windshield and brass fittings, including the lamps and radiator shell, make this a truly beautiful automobile.

It is a little difficult to see the car in this photograph, but it is a 1905 Rambler Surrey Type One. This press release photograph is for the 1949 movie *A Connecticut Yankee in King Arthur's Court*, based on the novel by Mark Twain. The man in the cap is, of course, Bing Crosby, the star of the picture. He plays a singing mechanic who finds himself suddenly in Arthurian England.

The 1905 Rambler Surrey Type Two was a perfect car "For the Theatre or Evening Use," according to this ad. Seating five people in beautifully upholstered comfort, the Rambler included roll-down side curtains in case of rain.

1905 Rambler-Surrey Type I

The Surrey Type One had a more conventional folding top, rather than the fixed roof seen on the Type Two. It was powered by a two-cylinder engine and was capable of traveling 35 miles per hour. These gentlemen appear to be taking part in some sort of racing or rally competition.

Three

1906–1913

The most expensive "open car" in the 1906 Rambler line-up was the Model 15, seen here. The factory described it as "A large and powerful touring car with a four-cylinder vertical motor, 35-40-hp." Riding a generous 112-inch wheelbase, the Model 15 could carry five passengers at speeds up to 50 miles per hour. The transmission was a three-speed sliding-gear unit, a type which was becoming increasingly popular with motorists.

The new Model 14 for 1906, priced at a reasonable $1,750 with full equipment, was a medium-weight touring car powered by a 20–25-horsepower, four-cylinder engine. An important innovation seen on Ramblers was the safety crank, a design that prevented the sudden recoil of the starting crank, which often occurred on early automobiles when the engine backfired while being cranked. With other cars, this could easily lead to a broken arm, but not on the Rambler!

Here is a profile view of the Model 15 for 1906. Note the strong yet graceful lines of the body. Its $2,500 price included gas headlights with a generator, side oil lamps, tail lamps, horn, wrenches, tire pump, and repair kit. Many of these items cost extra on other cars.

A party of travelers is all set to head out on a trip in their 1906 Rambler Surrey in Arthur, Illinois. More than 2,700 Ramblers were sold during the year.

1906 Rambler - Model 16

AMH-61-108

The 1906 Rambler Model 16 was a big, expensive car. A beautifully finished limousine with a fully enclosed rear compartment and partially enclosed driver's compartment, it was priced at $3,000. Powered by a 35–40-horsepower, four-cylinder engine, it rode a 112-inch wheelbase.

Rambler
Model 24

For the 1907 model year, Ramblers received several engineering upgrades and were given new model designations. The Model 24 shown here corresponded to the prior year's Model 14 but boasted a two-inch-longer wheelbase and a more powerful engine.

This is the Rambler Model 24 for 1907, which was new this year. It targeted a niche between the Models 21/22 and Model 25. Riding a 108-inch wheelbase, power was supplied by a 30-horsepower, four-cylinder engine. The vehicle shown has apparently been modified by the fitting of a larger windshield. Note, too, that the headlamps are missing.

There were several two-cylinder Rambler models for 1907. This Model 27 Roadster was the least expensive Rambler that year, with a price of just $950. In this press photograph, the company proudly displays one of Rambler's unique innovations: a side-hinged body that could be lifted up for easier servicing of the chassis.

Model 27, Price $950.

Equipped with acetylene head lamps with separate generator,
oil tail lamp, and 6-volt 60-ampere storage battery, $1,000.

The ideal qualities of a touring runabout are reached in the
Rambler Model 27.

In this is embodied the new Rambler unit power plant comprising a double opposed horizontal motor, planetary transmission
and multiple disc clutch entirely enclosed with three-point support.

No moving part of the motor or transmission gear is exposed,
and every part is entirely accessible from above.

You will not appreciate the many valuable features of this model
without our new catalogue containing complete description of this and
other 1907 models.   Mailed upon request.

Main Office and Factory, Kenosha, Wis., U. S. A.

Branches:

Chicago,   Milwaukee,   Boston,   Philadelphia,   San Francisco.
New York Agency, 38-40 W. 62nd St.   Representatives in all leading cities.

Thomas B. Jeffery & Company

Here is a factory advertisement for the 1907 Model 27 showing off the very stylish lines of what
the company termed "a touring runabout." The text notes that "every part is entirely accessible
from above" but fails to mention the tilting body that makes the excellent accessibility possible.
Note that the price is $50 higher when ordered with head lamps, acetylene generator, oil tail
lamp, and six-volt battery.

Rambler

Model 21, Price $1,350

The Most Efficient Car of Its Type Ever Built

The Rambler Model 21—the logical result of seven years of scientific development of the simple power plant.

In this car a double opposed motor, multiple disc clutch and planetary transmission are entirely enclosed as an integral unit with three-point support.

Accessibility is carried to a point never before acquired—the tilting body and constructive design enables every working part to be easily and entirely reached from above.

Write today for our catalogue describing this, our new runabout and two four-cylinder touring cars. It will give you information you ought to have before buying a car.

Main Office and Factory, Kenosha, Wis., U. S. A.

Branches:

Chicago,   Milwaukee,   Boston,   Philadelphia,   San Francisco.
New York Agency, 38-40 W. 52d Street.   Representatives in all leading cities.

Thomas B. Jeffery & Company

When Writing to Advertisers, Please Mention Motor Age.

With a price of just $1,350, the Rambler Model 21 for 1907 offered rare value in a motorcar. Its 100-inch wheelbase was long enough to accommodate the handsome four-to-five passenger touring body, and its two-cylinder engine provided enough power for comfortable cruising at reasonable speeds, along with excellent fuel economy. And perhaps most importantly, the Rambler was well known for reliability and quality of construction.

1907 RAMBLER, Model 25 — Wm. Jennings Bryan
shaking hands with George W. Peck (standing),
author of "Peck's Bad Boy"

AMH-64-358

Here is a rather interesting press photograph. The car is a 1907 Rambler Model 25, the most expensive Rambler that year, with a price of $2,500. The man standing at the rear of the car shaking hands with a gentleman seated in the rear is George W. Peck, author of *Peck's Bad Boy*. The man he is greeting in the car is the famous American politician William Jennings Bryan, a three-time candidate for the presidency of the United States.

907 Rambler

Two couples are about to embark on a day of fun in their 1907 Rambler touring car. Note the extravagant dusters the two front passengers are wearing; these were necessary in the early days of the automobile because most of America's roads were dirt, and cars kicked up quite a bit of dust as they motored along. The man standing outside the car is carrying a bag of golf clubs. With the advent of cars, it was easier for people to take advantage of leisure time to enjoy outdoor pursuits.

Details Make The Car

In The Model 24

Rambler

is every feature that makes mechanical excellence and general attractiveness.

Constructive Details

Motor—four-cylinder verticle, 4½ inch bore, 4½ inch stroke that gives full 25-30 horse power at the road wheels.

Transmission—sliding gear of a special type in which all trouble in shifting gears is absolutely avoided.

Final drive—propeller shaft and bevel gears with floating type rear axle fitted with ball and roller bearings throughout. Wheel base—108 inches, wheels 34 inch with 4 inch tires.

All accessories, such as mechanical sight feed lubricator, circulating pump, ignition timer, etc., are of the latest and most approved types.

Equipment includes full cape top, five lamps, horn, tools, storage battery, etc.

Price, as above, $2000.

Our catalogue, describing this and five other models—$950 to $2500—is at your service.

Main Office and Factory, Kenosha, Wisconsin

Branches:

Chicago, Milwaukee, Boston, Philadelphia, San Francisco.
New York Agency, 38-40 West 62nd Street. Representatives in all leading cities.

Thomas B. Jeffery & Company

The Rambler logo was well known in the United States because it had been used on the immensely popular Rambler bicycles for years before the introduction of the Rambler car. Shown is a 1907 Rambler Model 24, priced at $2,000 and offering a 25–30-horsepower engine, three-speed sliding gear transmission, and plenty of room for five passengers.

The Thomas B. Jeffery Co. factory was one of the best equipped in the country, and the firm made nearly every part of its cars, including bodies. In this photograph, taken inside the factory during 1907, workmen are busy providing finishing touches to touring car and limousine bodies. As closed cars began to become more popular, Jeffery sourced many of them from nearby Seaman Body Company in Milwaukee.

In this photograph, taken inside the Thomas B, Jeffery assembly plant in 1907, new automobiles are near the end of the assembly process and ready for shipping. Jeffery's factory was an almost completely self-contained operation and boasted a body shop, forge shop, engine plant, and upholstery department.

A Leader of Leaders

Model 25, the leader of the Rambler line for 1907, stands without a superior in comfort, convenience and positive dependability.

The mechanical equipment contains every feature that affords satisfaction to owner and operator, either for city service or long, continuous tours under most severe conditions.

See it and be convinced, or, if inconvenient to visit our nearest representative, write for our new catalogue describing this and three other models, each the leader in its respective class.

Main Office and Factory, Kenosha, Wisconsin

BRANCHES:

Boston   Chicago   Milwaukee   Philadelphia   San Francisco

Thomas B. Jeffery & Company

Model 25,
35-40 H.P.,
$2,500

The most expensive Rambler touring car in 1907 was the big Model 25, which weighed some 2,600 pounds and included a more powerful 35–40-horsepower engine. The price on this elegant machine was a very reasonable $2,500.

In most factories of the era, power was generated on site and got to the individual machine via a complex system of overhead shafts powering drive belts attached to each worker's machine. All the moving parts meant that one had to exercise caution while working or a hand or arm might get caught up in one of the moving belts and crushed. Jeffery was considered one of the most completely equipped automotive factories in the country.

This photograph of a 1908 Rambler tourer does not indicate which particular model it is, but it is most likely a Model 34 four-to-five-passenger touring car. The Model 34 rode a 112-inch wheelbase and was powered by a four-cylinder engine providing 32 horsepower. This car has had the headlamps and windshield frame removed.

Jeffery was one of the few early automobile manufacturers that regularly tested its cars for power, quality, and reliability. In this test, conducted at the plant's testing grounds, a Rambler chassis is driven up a 30-percent grade to test its power and climbing ability. In the early days of the automobile, an ability to climb steep hills was a real asset and selling feature.

In another view of Jeffery's testing methods, a factory hand runs a Rambler chassis on a public road loaded down with sandbags to test its strength and see how well it would perform when overloaded. In this era, it was not uncommon for automakers to test new products on public roads.

Model 34-A, $2,250.

The Ideal Transportation

The gentleman's roadster is the ideal connection between the suburban home and city office. It changes the hot, dusty journey on a crowded "local" to a pleasant ride in the clear, fresh air that fits you for the business of the day.

The Rambler roadster, Model 34-A., is a speedy, classy car with the power and endurance of a touring car and the convenience of a runabout.

Mechanically it possesses every valuable feature found in any car at any price, such as offset crank shaft, straight line drive, large wheels, etc., and in appearance has a distinctive character of its own that marks it a thoroughbred.

An examination will convince that

It is the Right Car at the Right Price

Two other models, touring cars at $1,400 and $2,250.
Our catalog gives full details, write for it today.

Thomas B. Jeffery & Company

Main Office and Factory, Kenosha, Wisconsin.

Branches and Distributing Agencies:
Chicago, Milwaukee, Boston, Philadelphia, San Francisco. Representatives in all leading cities.

When you write. please mention the Cosmopolitan

Here is an early Rambler advertisement that appeared in *Cosmopolitan* magazine. It shows the Rambler Model 34-A for 1908. Many reference books do not mention the Model 34-A, which was a four-cylinder roadster. The flared front fenders were useful on very muddy roads. Priced at $2,250, it was described as "a speedy, classy car with the power and endurance of a touring car and the convenience of a runabout." Standard colors for this model were a grey body and red wheels.

Here is another Model 34-A with noted Kenosha surgeon Dr. George Ripley at the wheel. This photograph appeared in the Rambler sales catalog that year. The good doctor was out for some early morning goose hunting. The right-hand steering, a feature of all Ramblers back then, was common in the US auto industry.

A larger, more substantial automobile was this 1908 Rambler Model 34, a four-cylinder car on a 112-inch wheelbase. The factory finish on the Model 34 was a maroon body with red wheels. These cars were extremely popular and enjoyed a reputation for excellent performance.

Here is the elegant Rambler Model 36 for 1908. The Model 36 was a five-passenger limousine weighing about 3,000 pounds and bearing a price tag of $3,250 F.O.B. from Kenosha (which meant that the buyer paid the shipping cost), making it both the heaviest and costliest Rambler that year. In fact, the price was $1,050 more than the next most expensive car in the line, the Rambler Model 345 Touring Car.

The year and model of this car are not exactly certain, but an educated guess is that this is a 1908 Rambler Model 34-A Roadster. The car appears to be a test unit, as it lacks fenders, running boards, hood, and head lamps. The mud spatters on the side are a clear indication that this is not an advertising photograph. The driver is not identified.

Here is another rather interesting photograph. The car is a 1908 Rambler Model 34 Touring Car. The man in the light-colored suit seated in the back is the great American author Mark Twain. This photograph appeared that year in the *Rambler Magazine*, a publication produced by the factory and sent to Rambler owners across the country. Rambler sales for 1908 totaled 3,597 vehicles.

This rare photograph again looks inside the Jeffery factory, this time in the department that produced seat frames for the Rambler automobiles. The company employed thousands of workers, including a great many highly skilled woodworkers like these.

THE CAR OF STEADY SERVICE

As
Applied
to
the

Is more than a mere phrase. It is a title earned through correct design and careful construction, and proven by years of hard, constant service wherever power-driven vehicles are known.

THE PRACTICAL QUALITIES THAT ESTABLISHED THE RAMBLER REPUTATION ARE:

1st   **APPLIED POWER.** By this we mean actual tractive force as applied to the road wheels. Owing to the straight line drive of the four-cylinder models, and the direct chain drive in the two-cylinder cars, Ramblers have greater propelling force per pound than any other car on the market.

2d   **DEPENDABILITY.** Ramblers are built to stand the test of hard, daily service over the worst of American roads. This condition is not reached by mere weight and masses of metal, but by simple, scientific construction in which each element is stronger than the strains upon it can ever require.

3d   **PRACTICAL ROAD VALUE.** With the vast facilities of an enormous plant like the Rambler factory, skilfully directed to the production of two models only, greater value per dollar can be offered than is possible in a plant of lesser output.

In short, the Rambler is a car of

POWER, SERVICE and VALUE

ORDINARY BUSINESS POLICY DICTATES A CAREFUL EXAMINATION OF ITS MANY HIGH QUALITIES BEFORE ORDERING YOUR NEW CAR

Our 1908 Catalog, fully describing two Touring Cars and a High-Powered Roadster, is at your service. WRITE TODAY

**MODEL 34-A
$2250**

THOMAS B. JEFFERY & COMPANY
Main Office and Factory
KENOSHA, WIS.

Branches and Distributing Agencies:—CHICAGO   MILWAUKEE   BOSTON   PHILADELPHIA   SAN FRANCISCO
REPRESENTATIVES IN ALL LEADING CITIES

When Writing to Advertisers, Please Mention Motor Age.

This advertisement that appeared in the January 30, 1908, issue of *The Motor* magazine, gives the main Rambler slogan for the year, "The Car of Steady Service." It was no empty boast: Ramblers were among the most dependable cars on the market, and their owners were highly loyal to the brand. The Model 34-A shown was a four-cylinder roadster on a long 112-inch wheelbase and priced at a lofty $2,250. The added rear seat was often referred to as a "mother-in-law" seat.

The 1909 Rambler touring car shown in this photograph is a Model 41. This press photograph was taken to demonstrate another clever Rambler innovation: a rear-hinged body mounted on springs that could be tilted upward to facilitate servicing the chassis. Similar to the earlier side-hinged design, the rear hinging allowed servicing from either side of the car.

The car in this photograph is a 1909 Rambler Model 41. The Model 41 was a light, 22-horsepower, two-cylinder touring car for town and country use. It rode a compact 106-inch wheelbase. The price was a very reasonable $1,350.

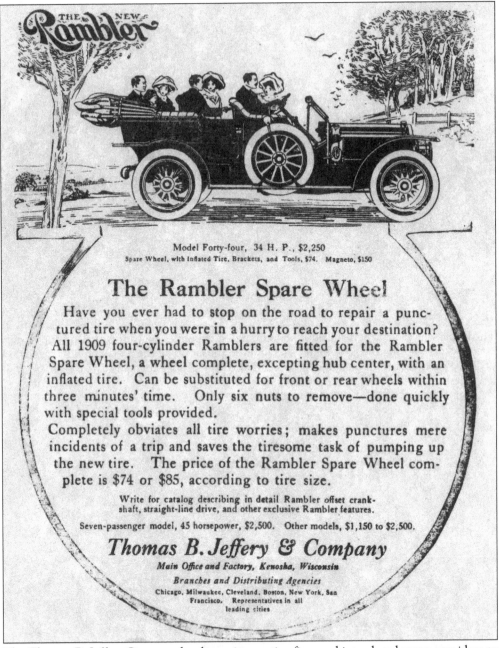

The Thomas B. Jeffery Co. proved to be an innovative firm and introduced many new ideas to the automotive industry. Perhaps its most ubiquitous and longest-lasting idea was the spare wheel and tire. In the earliest days of the auto industry, flat tires were a common occurrence because of the primitive technology and the rough, mostly unpaved roads. Motorists always carried a flat repair kit with them when they ventured out on the road because punctures were frequent. Jeffery introduced the idea of carrying a spare wheel and tire on the car so that flats could be swapped out rather than having to be fixed on the spot. This meant the motorist could quickly continue on his way. The motorist's flat could thus be repaired later in the comfort of his own garage rather than out in the elements.

The idyllic scene shown here includes a handsome 1909 Rambler touring car and a happy family of picnickers enjoying the great outdoors. However, the clarity of the photograph seems to be a little too good for 1909. The author suspects that this staged photograph was taken some years later, perhaps in the 1940s, for advertising purposes.

A c. 1909 Rambler touring car is pictured. Unfortunately, neither the driver and passengers nor the location are identified.

PRESIDENT TAFT IN RAMBLER AFTER GAME OF
GOLF AT COUNTRY CLUB, AUGUSTA, GA,

Here is another celebrity shown with a Rambler. The gentleman with the light-colored cap seated in the back of this 1910 Rambler Model 55 Touring Car is William Howard Taft, the 27th president of the United States. The picture was taken in Augusta, Georgia, on November 8, 1909, as Taft and friends were leaving the home of a Major Cummings.

Another view shows President Taft seated in the rear in a light-colored suit in the same Rambler Model 55 seen on the previous page.

The driver of this custom-built Rambler, Frank W. Wentworth, was a prominent club man in Chicago. He ordered this car, his eighth Rambler, built with a special retractable top that endowed it with very luxurious styling.

Will M. Cressy, shown at the wheel of his 1910 Rambler Model 55, was a famous vaudeville entertainer who often teamed up with his wife, Blanche Dayne. He was also a writer, and his screenplay credits include 1915's *Fifty Dollars a Kiss* and *Stateroom Secrets*, which debuted in 1919.

This handsome automobile is a 1910 Rambler Model 53 two-passenger touring car, which the factory described as having pleasing lines and features while providing unusual power, comfort, silence, and quality. Power came from a 34-horsepower engine. Riding a generous 109-inch wheelbase, the Model 53's factory colors were a Brewster green body and cream wheels. The base price was $1,800; top and side curtains were $75 extra, and a windshield was $40.

Here is the shipping room in the vast Jeffery factory in Kenosha. Note the belt-drives in the background. In this period, factories often used a single power source that provided power to overhead belts and pulleys, which then could be hooked in to power specific machinery.

Tom Jeffery took a well-deserved vacation in 1910, traveling to Egypt, Italy, and elsewhere. Here he is on the right in a dark suit, hat in hand, posing by the Sphinx and the Great Pyramid. Sadly, Tom Jeffery died while in Pompeii, Italy, during this trip.

This lovely drawing was the cover of a 1911 issue of the popular *Rambler Magazine* and is typical of the sort of artwork used in each issue. The covers generally featured idealized scenes drawn by artists, while inside the book was primarily articles illustrated by black-and-white photographs. The articles usually covered trips or adventures by Rambler owners and sometimes covered useful product information.

Early motorists were usually tourists, as opposed to how cars are used today as primary transportation. Here is a delightful scene as a group of tourists drives through a pretty little wood, probably in search of the ideal picnic spot. The Rambler is equipped with a folding top in case inclement weather shows up, and it carries a spare wheel and tire in case of a flat.

RAMBLER SIXTY-FOUR EQUIPPED FOR BAD WEATHER WITH STORM CURTAINS AND WIND SHIELD

Press photographs of early cars with weather protection fully installed and erected are few, but here is an excellent example. This is a 1911 Rambler Model 64 Touring Car with its top erected and side curtains installed, providing nearly perfect protection from rain or snow, though visibility is admittedly somewhat restricted. Once such protection became common, it was not long before onboard heaters came into use to keep motorists warm as well as dry. The Model 64 boasted a 120-inch wheelbase.

This c. 1911 photograph shows a typical farming scene of the day with a crew of farmhands harvesting and baling hay. The Rambler appears to be a Model 64 of 1911 vintage.

When the C.I. Terwilliger & Son firm of Port Jervis, New York, decided it needed a truck for its growing business, it chose to have one built on a standard Rambler Model 63 Roadster. The Model 63 rode a 112-inch wheelbase and featured a 34-horsepower, four-cylinder engine, so it was ideal for a light, economical service vehicle. Note how the long bed extends well past the rear wheels.

The author has been unable to determine the exact model of the vehicle shown here. The photograph is labeled as a 1912 Rambler touring car, but no model number is mentioned. The front section features doors, unlike models of just a few years earlier that only included doors for the rear compartment.

In the 1940s and 1950s, executives at Nash-Kelvinator Corporation became increasingly interested in the full history of their company, including the period of time when it was the Thomas B. Jeffery Co. The company even purchased a few examples of vintage Rambler cars for use in displays. The very rare and handsome sedan seen here is a 1912 Rambler Knickerbocker. It was photographed outside Nash's Service Training Center during a dealer visit some time in the 1940s or early 1950s.

Another view shows the 1912 car above, joined now by a mint 1902 Rambler owned by Nash-Kelvinator. The men in this photograph are believed to be Nash service trainers and dealer mechanics. The author often wondered whatever became of this automobile, since it was not part of the collection acquired by Chrysler when it purchased American Motors in 1987. He has learned that it was donated by American Motors to the Henry Ford Museum and is currently in the latter's collection. It may well be the only surviving example of the Knickerbocker.

The Rambler Country Club, $2250

Beginning in 1912, the Jeffery company advertised model names rather than numbers. Seen here is a 1912 Rambler Country Club, a sharp touring car priced at $2,250.

Here is a Rambler Cross Country for 1912. The model colors are a bright red body with a black hood and red wheels. The car was named after an incident in which a Rambler owner chased a horse thief for many hours, driving cross country rather than sticking to roads. He eventually caught the man.

This elegant machine is the 1912 Rambler Gotham Limousine, which came from the factory finished in the buyer's choice of stylish colors: Brewster green, dark maroon, or Rambler blue, with harmonizing trim. The company described the Gotham as a "light limousine designed especially for city and suburban uses, but with ample power for touring." The Gotham was priced at a very reasonable $2,750. Total Rambler production for 1912 was 3,550 vehicles.

Although this 1912 Rambler Knickerbocker looks similar to the car above, their bodies are actually completely different. The Knickerbocker was a heavier, more powerful limousine for all-around use and boasted a 50-horsepower, four-cylinder engine. It was what the company termed a Berline-type vehicle, meaning it was a fully enclosed sedan as compared to the Gotham Limousine, which had a semi-open front compartment.

In addition to the two limousine types offered by the Thomas B. Jeffery Co. in 1912, there was also a shorter Rambler Sedan, targeted to women in this advertisement. It came with electric starting and full weather protection, two items the factory believed would appeal more to women than to men. The Rambler Sedan was priced at $2,500. An open Rambler Cross Country Touring Car was also available for $1,700.

Jeffery offered this snappy little Rambler Cross Country Roadster as part of its 1913 model lineup. Priced at $1,650, it was powered by a 38-horsepower, four-cylinder engine.

Here is the most popular Rambler for 1913, the Cross Country Touring Car, also known as the Model 83. In a display of the faith the company had in its products, this year, all new Ramblers were guaranteed by the factory for 10,000 miles, an outstanding warranty for the time.

In 1913, the Jeffery Company held a large parade of Rambler Cross Country cars. The vehicles were driven through Kenosha by the company's department foremen, though the reason for the parade is unknown.

A 1913 Model 83 Rambler Cross Country Touring Car is seen here picking up passengers for a pleasure drive out to the country. The finish was the ever-popular Brewster green body with black fenders and hood with gold pinstripes. The company had a good year in 1913, producing 4,435 cars and 5,578 trucks.

Four

1914–1916

After selling automobiles under the Rambler brand for 12 years, the Thomas B. Jeffery Co. decided to switch to the Jeffery name for its products. According to the company, this was to honor the founder, who had died four years earlier, though it should be noted that Jeffery was also the name of his successors. As a marketing decision, it was a mistake, because the Rambler brand had an excellent, worldwide reputation; the Jeffery name was less well known. A smarter approach would have been to add a second line of high-end cars bearing the Jeffery name while retaining the Rambler name for the volume-selling cars. The vehicle pictured is a 1914 Jeffery Four All-Weather Coupe

This detail photograph of the interior of a Jeffery Four Touring Car shows central placement of the gauges. Note that steering is on the left-hand side, and that the clutch pedal bears a large letter C, while the brake pedal has a letter B. Controls on automobiles had not yet been standardized, so labeling them helped drivers.

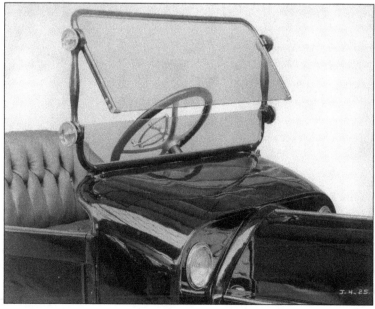

A close-up photograph of the windshield details on the 1914 Jeffery Four Touring Car shows that part of the glass could be folded forward to provide drivers with a cooling breeze.

The popular 1914 Jeffery Four Touring Car was a roomy and comfortable automobile with a price tag of $1,450. The car featured a 38-horsepower engine and electric starting.

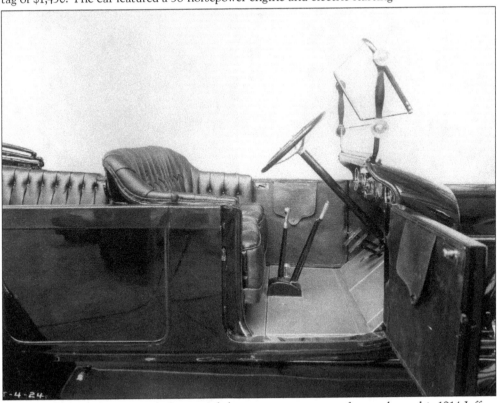

Note the high-quality seat upholstery and the neat arrangement of controls on this 1914 Jeffery automobile. The company took great pride in its workmanship.

With war raging in Europe, the Thomas B. Jeffery Co. began to experiment with military vehicles, including the armored car shown here. Inspecting the vehicle is Harold Jeffery; this is one of the few photographs of him the author has been able to locate.

This is another version of the Jeffery armored vehicle. Both vehicles were taken to Mexico during Gen. John Pershing's attempt to bring Pancho Villa and his revolutionaries to justice. The Jeffery vehicles performed well but were never put into series production.

This 1914 Jeffery Six Roadster was specially built for racing. Note the fully open body and the lack of a windshield.

This large vehicle is a 1914 Jeffery with a specially built hearse body. The coach lamps, engraved glass panels, and window curtains lend it the proper air of solemnity.

Pictured here is another 1914 Jeffery commercial car, this one a taxicab. The driver is protected from the weather by a roof and doors and could fit plastic side curtains if needed. Passengers had full-weather protection but could also enjoy top-down motoring if desired. Note the taxi meter.

The 1914 Jeffery taxi is the same car as above but now has the rear roof folded down for fresh-air motoring.

The Jeffery Four touring car for 1914 is pictured.

Seen here is a 1914 Jeffery Four Model 93A, an all-weather coupe with folding top. The oval side window is a nice styling touch that provides better visibility than the blind quarters seen on many convertible coupes.

Jeffery Four Roadster, Two Passenger, $1,550

In every town there is a man or woman recognized for individuality of taste. We have built to please that individual the most distinguished, up-to-the-minute Roadster in America. It's an exclusive car for people who will have only the latest. The extra wheel and tire are carried under the rear deck, which can be raised as neatly as you please. Wire wheels extra, and they are the best that money can buy.

The car pictured here is a 1914 Jeffery Four Model 93 Roadster, a fairly basic car with a price of $1,550. A two-passenger job, it was powerful enough for touring. Included was a spare wheel and tire mounted under the deck lid.

This 1914 Jeffery fire truck was specially built on a medium-duty Jeffery truck chassis.

Looking nearly identical to the Jeffery Four Roadster, save for the longer hood, is this 1914 Jeffery Six Model 96 Roadster, also a two-passenger car but much smoother and more powerful. The price for this car was $2,250.

Here is a very famous vehicle—the Jeffery Quad truck. Originally developed in 1913, it was one of the earliest four-wheel-drive trucks built and boasted four-wheel brakes and four-wheel steering as well. The Quad was one of the toughest trucks ever built and was well received by the public.

This rugged-looking machine is a 1914 Jeffery Quad fitted with an express delivery body. Note the solid steel wheels.

Few early trucks could go places that a Quad could. With its four-wheel drive and tremendous pulling power, it was a natural for logging companies.

In the early days of motoring, sedans were expensive and therefore sold in lower volume than touring cars. But this great-looking 1914 Jeffery Four Model 93 Sedan offered excellent protection from the weather and was priced at a reasonable $2,350.

The four-cylinder engine used in the Jeffery Four was compact, efficient, reliable, and offered 40 horsepower. The company produced its own engines in-house, unlike dozens of other companies that purchased engines from outside suppliers.

Three views of the Jeffery four-cylinder engine illustrate its compact, efficient design.

The Jeffery Quad truck could be fitted with just about any kind of work body needed. The one shown here appears to be an ambulance.

Note the heavy-duty, solid-steel wheels on this c. 1914 Jeffery Quad truck. This particular truck is fitted with a grain body with flare boards but without any sort of cab enclosure.

Seen here is a Jeffery Quad truck with a basic cab enclosure, known as a "C-cab" because of the shape of the side panel. It is also fitted with headlamps and a central driving lamp for extra night-time vision. The work body has not yet been fitted to this vehicle.

Big things were happening at Jeffery in 1915. The company launched a new line of six-cylinder automobiles named the Jeffery Chesterfield Six. This stylish touring car was probably the most popular of the new Sixes.

Here is the Jeffery Chesterfield Six Touring Car for 1915 with the top up. Side curtains could be fitted to provide all-weather protection. This year, the Jeffery company was focusing most of its attention on truck production. War was raging across Europe, and there was a strong need for Jeffery Quad trucks, because their power and four-wheel-drive capability made them ideal for hauling guns and supplies.

In addition to its Quad line of trucks, Jeffery also produced this light roadster pickup for 1915. The tire chains on the rear wheels improved traction in the snow. Note the cargo!

Another Jeffery truck is shown here, a 1915 model fitted with an express delivery body. It was purchased by the C&P Telephone Company (probably the Chesapeake & Potomac).

Here is a 1915 Jeffery Model 93-2 Chesterfield Four, which had a retail price of just $1,500. Jeffery's advertising manager was a young man named Ned Jordan, who would go on to create some of the most famous ads of all time.

This handsome sedan is a 1915 Jeffery Chesterfield Model 104, priced at $2,450 and a very nice automobile for the money. One Jeffery ad this year depicted a young woman smoking a cigarette; it is said to be the first automobile ad to do so.

The JEFFERY SIX-48 Approves

Jeffery

The Thomas B. Jeffery Company
Kenosha, Wis. U.S.A.

U P-TO-DATENESS has always been the keynote of the Jeffery policy, a state of preparedness which has won for the Thomas B. Jeffery Company a prominent place in the front rank of automobile manufacturers.

It has enabled them to employ many vital improvements long before other manufacturers had even started to investigate the merits of those same improvements.

Constant research and long experience breed a keen discrimination. We, therefore, with justifiable pride, make the announcement that after painstaking investigation The Thomas B. Jeffery Company has adopted

The Vulcan Electric Gear Shift

as special equipment on the Jeffery Six-48 at an additional list price of $150.

According to this advertisement from the *Automobile Trade Journal*, the Jeffery Six-48 for 1915 offered the Vulcan electric gear shift, which automated some of the shift functions.

Pictured is the Jeffery Chesterfield Four Touring Car for 1915. On May 2 of that year, Charles Jeffery set sail for England, where he planned to study the latest innovations in automobile manufacturing and design. However, the ship he booked passage on was the ill-fated *Lusitania*, which was torpedoed by a German U-boat 11 miles off the coast of Ireland. The ship sank in less than 20 minutes, and most of its passengers drowned. However, Jeffery's wife had made him promise to keep a life preserver in his cabin, and in the end, it saved his life. Jeffery spent four hours in the water before being rescued.

Niagara
Camp,
1915

Jimmy Mess (in centre) Eaton M.G. Battery

Shown here is one of the Jeffery armored cars at Camp Niagara in 1915. Camp Niagara was a large training camp used by the military during the Great War.

This modern photograph of one of the Jeffery armored cars seems to indicate that at least one of the vehicles has survived to the present. However, the location where the photograph was taken is unknown at this time.

The Thomas B. Jeffery Co. concentrated its efforts primarily on trucks this year, selling 7,600 units versus 3,100 cars. This is the 1915 Jeffery Model 96-2 Roadster.

Equipped with a special paddy wagon body, this 1915 Jeffery police vehicle was ideal for bringing in crooks and troublemakers. Note the large bell just behind the door.

The Jeffery company introduced several new models for 1916, including this sharp Jeffery Four Model 462-5. The final digit in the model number indicates that it is a five-passenger automobile. Note the Goodyear tires fitted to this car.

This photograph bears no identification but is believed to show a 1916 Jeffery Four Model 462-7, which would make it a seven-passenger touring car. The short hood seems to verify that it is a Four, while the jump seats visible in the rear indicate its seven-passenger carrying capacity.

Looking very elegant is this 1916 Jeffery Four Sedan. Jeffery offered its four-cylinder sedans in both five- and seven-passenger versions. Although the photograph is not marked with any identification, this car appears to be a seven-passenger model.

Large and powerful-looking, this stylish car is a 1916 Jeffery Model 661 Touring. Rated as a seven-passenger car, it was perfect for large families and long journeys. This big six-cylinder automobile could be purchased for a mere $1,450, a lower price than the four-cylinder Jeffery sold for just two years earlier. It was the result of an industry-wide trend: as car production increased, so did production efficiency and competition, the net effect of which was a sharp reduction in prices.

Make Certain of *Your* Jeffery Now

THE joys of Jeffery ownership are not for everybody this year—a Jeffery shortage is an assured fact.

Now, when Nature is just beginning to smile, is the time to assure yourself this privilege, and throughout all the golden days of Spring and Summer you will realize to the full your perfect satisfaction in your purchase.

Your judgment in selecting the car which introduced the high-speed, long-stroke, high-efficiency motor to America will be justified daily by actual performance in comparison with the products of other factories which have followed the Jeffery example.

From radiator to rear axle you will find a multitude of other evidences of Jeffery leadership—made possible because the car has been developed by Jeffery engineers, and is built, practically in its entirety, in the Jeffery factory. You will be satisfied with the car as a unit because the car has been built as a unit to satisfy you.

An early visit to your Jeffery dealer will insure *you* this satisfaction—and at the very time of the year when motoring is most delightful.

THE JEFFERY FOUR		THE NEW JEFFERY SIX	
Seven Passenger Touring	$1035	A light-weight Six, of distinctive beauty and sur-	
Without auxiliary seats	1000	passing comfort — with practically unlimited	
Three Passenger Roadster	1000	power and speed.	
Sedan—top removable, summer top included	1165	(Prices F. O. B. Kenosha, Wis.)	$1450

BOOKLET ON REQUEST

The Thomas B. Jeffery Company
Main Office and Works, Kenosha, Wisconsin

This lovely advertisement illustrates the large size and fine styling of the 1916 Jeffery automobile and calls attention to the fact that Jefferys were selling faster than the factory could build them. Charles Jeffery was more interested in producing quality rather than quantity.

The Jeffery Four

"America's Standard Automobile at a $1000 Price"

People who formerly paid $2000 to $5000 for an automobile now find the very qualities they have always insisted upon —in the Jeffery Four, at $1000.

Body, standard seven-passenger Chesterfield type · Front seats, divided · Driver's seat, adjustable · Upholstery, deep real leather · Shipping weight, 2750 pounds · Motor, Jeffery high-speed high-efficiency · Ignition, Bosch magneto · Starting and lighting system, Bijur electric · Equipment, complete · Entire car 93% Jeffery-built.

STANDARD SEVEN-PASSENGER, $1035; *without Auxiliary Seats,* $1000 · THREE-PASSENGER ROADSTER, $1000
SEDAN (*Removable Top*) $1165 · JEFFERY SIX, $1350

Prices F.O.B. Kenosha, Wisconsin

The Thomas B. Jeffery Company
Main Office and Works · Kenosha, Wisconsin

Illustrated booklet on request

Jeffery prices for 1916 began at $1,000 for a four-cylinder roadster or standard touring car without jump seats. The cars represented a tremendous value because of their superior build quality and level of standard features.

The Jeffery touring car for 1916 is pictured with two lovely ladies out for a drive.

This lovely little machine is the Jeffery four-cylinder Roadster for 1916, a car with sporty lines and a low price of just $1,000.

In 1916, Jeffery focused much attention on the capabilities of the Quad trucks. Here is one operated by a lumber and coal company. The Quad could easily carry a heavy load of lumber, as shown here.

Hauling heavy steel pipes was another easy job for the extra-heavy-duty Quad. In this photograph, a trailer has been added to help handle the extra length of the pipes.

Some men claimed that the Quad truck was so powerful it could pull a house. The two gentlemen seen here proved the point. The Quad was capable of amazing feats.

Here is another Quad in the service of a fuel and lumber company, this one the F.R. Brumwell Company in Huron, South Dakota. The owner wisely had the Quad fitted with a fully enclosed cab for protection from the harsh South Dakota winters.

The huge steel gear wheel seen in this photograph had to be delivered to a company. The owner of the Quad used the power of his truck to pull the gear wheel onto a heavy-duty platform trailer, which could then be pulled by the Quad.

Here is the complete outfit with the gear wheel on the trailer, all hooked up to the Quad for transport to the end-user. The Quad was one of the few trucks available back then that could do this sort of hauling.

Not surprisingly, the Jeffery Quad trucks were popular for highway construction projects. In 1916, Jeffery was awarded large orders for Quads by the US military as well as from its allies.

This c. 1916 Jeffery fire truck was built on a heavy-duty Jeffery Quad truck chassis. During 1916, the president of General Motors, Charles William Nash, resigned his position and began looking for an automobile company to purchase. Nash wanted to produce an all-new car carrying his own name.

In response to acts of terrorism by Pancho Villa and his band of violent Mexican revolutionaries, who attacked the town of Columbus, New Mexico, killing 16 American citizens, the US government sent the Mexican Punitive Expedition, a military force led by Gen. John J. Pershing, with orders to capture or kill Villa and put a halt to his attacks. From March 1916 to February 1917, this force chased Villa throughout Northern Mexico. A column of Jeffery Quad trucks was taken along with the expedition in order to field test them under actual tactical situations.

The Jeffery Quad military trucks in the Mexican expedition were used to haul supply wagons and to carry heavy machine guns. This was the first use of motor truck convoys used in a military operation conducted by the US Army. The four-wheel-drive Quads proved unstoppable.

Jeffery Quad military trucks are pictured on duty during the Mexican Punitive Expedition. Testing these trucks in the field helped the Army to understand their special strengths, knowledge which proved very useful when the United States entered the First World War.

Although the big Quad trucks were rather slow moving, they could carry immense cargo weights with ease, allowing the expedition to carry a large quantity of munitions and food.

One side benefit of including the Jeffery Quad trucks on the Mexico expedition was that some of the soldiers could ride rather than march. These troopers are outfitted in the standard Army uniform of the time, which included boots, leggings, and broad-brimmed campaign hats.

Despite the desolate country in which the Army traveled, the Jeffery Quad trucks were able to operate easily due to their superior four-wheel-drive traction and immense pulling power. Interestingly, one of the units in the expedition was the US 7th Cavalry, which years earlier had been led by Col. George Armstrong Custer until he was killed in 1876 at the Battle of the Little Big Horn in Montana.

A Jeffery Quad is photographed in front of a general store in a small town in Mexico. A cab roof was required because of the intense heat in the Mexican desert.

Four Quads travel cross-country during the 1916–1917 Mexican expedition. General Pershing established his first base in Mexico at Colonia Dublan, a Mormon colony where George Romney, future head of American Motors, was born. Romney's family had been forced to flee the area some time earlier due to the back-and-forth battling of Mexican armed forces and revolutionaries.

The deep ruts seen here in the sandy Mexican scrubland offer mute testimony to the difficult travel conditions. Ordinary two-wheel-drive trucks would get stuck in such terrain.

Jeffery Quad trucks climb a steep grade off-road during the Mexico expedition of 1916–1917.

In 1916, Charles W Nash resigned his position as president of General Motors in order to go into business for himself as an automaker. After attempting to buy the Packard Motorcar Company, he and his associates purchased the Thomas B. Jeffery Co. and soon changed the name of the firm to the Nash Motors Company. Shown here is Nash, right, with Charles T. Jeffery, son of the founder and head of the Jeffery company. Charles Jeffery had been one of the fortunate survivors of the sinking of the *Lusitania*, but the experience changed him. Afterwards, he lost interest in business and chose to dedicate the rest of his life to quieter pursuits.

Five

1917–1918

Charles Nash was one of the most interesting businessmen of the 20th century. When he was just eight years old, his parents divorced, and young Charles was bound out by court order to do chores for a farmer in exchange for room and board. By the time he was 12 years old, he had run away and set out on his own, hiring out as a farm laborer. By dint of hard work and tremendous effort, he worked his way up the ladder of success, becoming a self-made millionaire. His rags-to-riches tale is still an inspiration. In this photograph, Nash is pictured in front of the former Jeffery building, now renamed the Nash Motors Company. He is in the very center of the first row, wearing a light suit and holding his arm to his waist.

Announcing the New Jeffery Six

A Triumph of Precision and Exquisite Performance!

In this new Jeffery Six are crystallized the ideals and traditions of two generations of accuracy.

Like its predecessors, it embodies those refinements of design and construction which mark it as a car of exceptional merit.

Its dominant features are a long, low, hammock-swung body and amazingly smooth performance.

The lowness of the body, with its underslung springs, gives the car a phenomenal

$1365

The New Jeffery Symbol

Upon each new Jeffery Six there appears the Jeffery device, shown above. It is more than a hall-mark —more than a trade-mark. It is the symbol of mechanical precision and refinement. It tokens the ideals of accuracy of the Jeffery organization. And as such it is the owner's guaranty of inherent worth, just as is the hall-mark upon the finished product of a maker of instruments of precision.

ability to cling to the road at high speeds. The oversized, inherently balanced crankshaft, with extra large bearings, is chiefly responsible for the fact that the motor is absolutely free from vibration at ALL speeds.

A beautiful car. The new, low, graceful lines and superb finish mark it as the greatest achievement of Jeffery coach builders.

The simplicity of the chassis and the performance of the motor are in a class by

(Continued on other side)

The sales piece shown here is for the new 1917 Jeffery Six series and is one of the last such fliers produced by the Thomas B. Jeffery Co. Once Charles Nash and his associates purchased the company, they changed the name to Nash Motors Company. However, the cars continued to be sold under the Jeffery name for a time.

Here is the cover of a very rare brochure for the 1917 Jeffery Six Model 671 seven-passenger touring car, which carried a price of $1,465. Inside the front of this brochure, the manufacturer is now listed as the Nash Motors Company. Charles Nash was originally attracted to Jeffery because of its reputation and its well-equipped factory, which produced nearly all the parts that went into the car.

Parlor Car Comfort

JUST as much as the car owner demands Jeffery power and safety, he desires Jeffery comfort. The vibrationless motor and the inherently balanced crankshaft are material forces in giving him his desire.

Factors as important are the springs of the Jeffery—extra strong, extra long, soft in action, easy-riding, *and flat under load.* Those in front are semi-elliptic, those in the rear ¾ *elliptic and underslung.*

They alone are sufficient to insure surpassing driving comfort and repose. And to them is added the divan type upholstery—real leather and real hair—*body-fitting, luxurious, deep.*

A big, roomy, comfortable seven passenger body—wide aisleway between front seats—auxiliary seats that disappear into the backs of the front seats.

5

Jeffery touring cars for 1917 were advertised as having "Parlor Car Comfort," a reference to the luxury train cars then in common use for long-distance travel. Jeffery cars continued to enjoy an outstanding reputation.

The Jeffery Six Roadster

is especially designed by the famous Jeffery engineers—to meet the demand of a large class of business men and women for a car for business purposes—a car which will exactly *fit* those purposes.

—for a car with unusual acceleration features, together with ample speed and power.

—for the large and important class of families who want a car which is roomy and comfortable.

—to satisfy the demand of enthusiastic Jeffery touring car owners for a roadster with the "stand up" quality, comfort, and motor of the Jeffery Six.

The Jeffery Six Sedan

Built for those who realize—that to use a car in winter is most uncomfortable unless one has protection from the weather and—that to obtain such protection one should not find it necessary to drive with a winter top during the summer.

The Jeffery Touring Car with demountable

Sedan top is the satisfactory solution of this problem. This car, with the Sedan top in place, is in appearance and luxury a perfect closed car of the finest type and with elegant appointments, yet when the bright days of Spring arrive the Sedan top can be quickly removed and the Summer top and windshield mounted in its place.

14

The 1917 Jeffery line also included this handsome six-cylinder roadster priced at a bargain $1,335 and the top-of-the-line Jeffery Six Model 671 Sedan, which carried a price tag of $1,530. These low prices were the result of greatly expanded production, according to the company.

The Jeffery Circle

Vol. 1, No. 6   PUBLISHED BY THE NASH MOTORS COMPANY, KENOSHA, WISCONSIN   OCTOBER

Factory Chiefs Powwow for Bigger Production

Output Boosters Meet Once Weekly

Foremen and Others Get Together and Work Out Production Plans and Solve Problems

"**C**ARS, cars—give us more cars!" being the universal cry of our dealers just now, it ought to interest them to know what the factory force is doing in the way of boosting production figures. A complete program is being mapped out and put into practice, directed by Mr. Nash himself. He spends hours daily in the factory.

Starting several weeks ago, we are holding regular Monday evening production meetings in the factory attended by the various department heads and foremen, with Mr. Nash handling the gavel. At these conferences current problems are brought up and discussed and viewed from every angle, and when the collection of aired ideas is complete some plan of action is evolved.

Co-operation, fellowship, loyalty, industry, singleness of purpose, smooth, cohesive efforts on the part of many men toward the same goal—these are but a few of the things that are bound to grow out of these powwows. Moreover, all are attended by our old friend, Henry J. Enthusiasm. In fact, he's the most conspicuous figure of all.

Every minute of these weekly confabs is taken up to advantage. Brass tacks, so called, are indulged in from opening to closing. One man gets up, introduces a knotty problem and sits down. Then everybody with a say says it. Pretty soon the knots in the problem are whittled away, and the solution stands out in bold relief. Next morning things are changed accordingly in the factory.

Pointers From Mr. Nash

Suggestions galore are furnished by Mr. Nash. Needless to say, the fellows directing the 3,000 trained hands in the shops are deriving inestimable benefit from Mr. Nash's own thorough experiences as a manufacturer—as the man whose methods built up General Motors to the point where it could report $29,000,000 as a single year's net profits.

Today we find a different spirit in the factory. Any lost motion that might have existed is being gradually eliminated. It is now only a matter of a short time before we will have the production up to big figures.

During the first meeting between Charles Nash, shown in front of his modest desk, and his factory managers, Nash declared that he was not interested in replacing the men with his own people. Nash realized the managers were well experienced and among the best men for each position. All he wanted to do, said Nash, was to increase production as quickly as possible using the methods he had developed over his long and successful career. Nash met with his managers every Monday evening to sort out production bottlenecks and solve any problems that might have appeared.

Here is the four-cylinder Jeffery Touring Car for 1917. A seven-passenger automobile, it carried a price of just $1,095 F.O.B from Kenosha.

In 1917, a Jeffery Touring Car climbed Pike's Peak, a heady display of its power and stamina. The mountain's promontory is so high that vegetation cannot grow, lending it an eerie, moon-like landscape.

Jeffery All-Purpose Truck busy day and night in the service of Dawson Brothers Manufacturing Company, Atlanta, Georgia. This truck has greatly reduced their haulage costs.

Buy Your Truck
to Fit Your Individual Needs

KEEPING the cost of deliveries cut to the minimum is the problem of every business executive. It adds dollars to the profit column at the end of the fiscal year.

Have you solved your haulage problems correctly? If your deliveries are to be made most efficiently, with greatest despatch and with least cost, it is all-important that your truck or fleet of trucks be adapted to your particular needs.

The Jeffery All-Purpose Truck is built for those businesses which require a truck of 3,000 pounds capacity. It is a sturdy, dependable vehicle which has proved its superiority in the hands of thousands of owners.

Let us diagnose your trucking needs. If a Jeffery All-Purpose Truck will not suit your particular requirement there is the Jeffery Rapid Service Wagon, 1,500 pounds capacity, and the famous Jeffery Quad for heavy duty, 4,000 pounds capacity.

6614 Jeffery Trucks In Service January 1, 1917

Not many photographs exist of the Jeffery All-Purpose trucks of 1917, but the author has been able to find a few. As this ad states, as of January 1917, there were 6,614 of these trucks in service, quite a good record.

One of the many lines of business in which the Jeffery All-Purpose Truck
has been used successfully is the Lumber Industry.

THE Jeffery All-Purpose Truck is giving rapid and dependable service in 55 lines of business. It is particularly well adapted for bakers, confectioners, bottlers and brewers, builders and contractors, bus-lines, creameries, department stores, express, grain-dealers, florists, commission men, furniture, groceries, hardware, laundries, lumber, publishers.

In fact any business requiring a sturdy, dependable truck with 3,000 pounds capacity and a speed of 16 miles per hour will find the Jeffery All-Purpose Truck efficient and economical.

Jeffery All-Purpose Truck
fitted out for fire protection,
Lisbon, North Dakota.

Fitted with standard Combination Chemicals and Hose, $2665
(Specifications on application)

6614 Jeffery Trucks In Service January 1, 1917

Two Jeffery trucks are shown here: a standard All-Purpose chassis fitted with an enclosed cab and lumber delivery body and an All-Purpose truck fitted with a fire truck body. Both bodies would have cost significantly extra and would have been produced by an outside supplier. The base cost of the Jeffery truck chassis was $1,465.

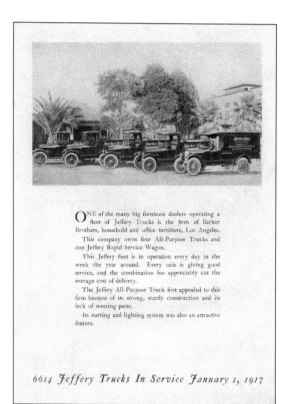

In addition to the All-Purpose
trucks, Jeffery also offered its
Rapid Service Wagon, seen at the
far right in this photograph.

Here is one of the rarest of all Jeffery
or Nash advertisements. Dated 1917, it
shows the Jeffery name superimposed
over the Nash Motors name, a signal
that the company had changed hands
and would soon change the name of
its products. The car itself is a Jeffery
Sedan with a price of $1,630. Charles
Nash was producing as many Jeffery
cars as he could to use up existing
stockpiles of parts and components,
which would clear the way for the all-
new car he would introduce under his
own name. The sprawling Nash-Jeffery
factory can be seen in the background.

The Jeffery Sedan, $1630

The car in this photograph is identified as a 1917 Nash Model 671. According to an early edition of the *Rambler Family Album*, an official publication of American Motors, some Jeffery automobiles were rebadged as Nashes, with few changes other than a revised radiator. Supposedly, Nash built these cars just prior to launching his own new car design. The statement does not appear in later versions of the *Family Album* and may be incorrect. This may simply be a Jeffery that has been misidentified as a transitional Nash.

This photograph has likewise been identified as showing a Jeffery rebadged as a Nash, but this is known to be incorrect, because the photograph appears in the all-new Nash Six catalog that year.

Quad truck production continued at the Kenosha plant. These are identified as Nash Quads, but it may simply be an earlier photograph of Jeffery Quads, since there are only minor differences in the two.

NASH QUAD
22 BALES OF COTTON
22 MILES IN 2 HOURS
22 MINUTES
MEMPHIS NASH MOTOR CO

In time, the Jeffery Quad became the Nash Quad, with revised radiator badging and minor improvements to the product. When large military orders were received, Nash became the largest truck manufacturer in America.

Once the Quad became a Nash model, the company changed the radiator to incorporate the Nash name, and in many instances displayed the Nash name on the side panels and anywhere else it could in order to rebrand the Quad in the public's mind.

It appears that the Jeffery All-Purpose trucks were dropped after a time, because Charles Nash introduced a new Nash One-Ton truck model; the Jeffery had been a one-and-a-half-ton model. The Nash One-Ton truck here is fitted out for military use, though for exactly what purpose is unknown.

On the left is a Nash One-Ton truck fitted with a dump body and a C-style cab, while on the right is a Nash Quad also outfitted with a dump body and C-cab.

Always innovative, Nash engineers produced this early tractor-trailer combination on a Nash One-Ton truck chassis.

This Nash One-Ton truck was ordered by the Standard Oil Company of Indiana for use in transporting fuel.

The iceman cometh. This c. 1917–1918 Nash One-Ton was fitted with an insulated body for use in home delivery of ice back in the days before electric refrigerators.

John the Coal Man bought this c. 1917 Nash One-Ton for his coal delivery business.

This Morris & Company Nash truck features a heavy-duty bed with flare boards, though what sort of product was carried is unknown.

ABOUT THE AUTHOR

One of America's best-known automotive writers is Patrick Foster, a dedicated historian and author whose career spans more than 25 years. Foster is a feature writer and has regular columns in *Hemmings Classic Car* and *Old Cars Weekly*. He has written 24 books and contributed to several others. Foster has won numerous awards including, the Antique Automobile Club of America's prestigious Thomas McKean Memorial Cup Award for the best book of automotive history for 1998. In 1997, one of his works was named Outstanding Periodical Article for the year by the Society of Automotive Historians. In 2011, Foster was honored with the Lee Iacocca Award, perhaps the most coveted in the car hobby, for excellence in automotive writing. The 2015 International Automotive Media Council (IAMC) Awards saw him bring home a silver medal for an article on 1930–1934 Nash automobiles and a bronze medal for his book *Jeep: The History of America's Greatest Vehicle*. In 2016, Foster took home two awards from the IAMC when *International Harvester Trucks: The Complete History* won a silver medal and an article on George Romney was awarded a bronze. In 2017, Foster won three awards in the IAMC competition, including gold medals for his books *Willys-Overland Illustrated History* and *Airstream: America's World Traveler*. Foster was also honored with the award for best book writing for the year.

Visit us at
arcadiapublishing.com

· ·

CPSIA information can be obtained
at www.ICGtesting.com
Printed in the USA
BVHW010903241022
650135BV00004B/178